POETIC MEMORIES

by Kathleen Morris

ISBN 978-1-927828-45-8

A NOTE FROM THE AUTHOR – These poems were
written in a span of twenty years. They were written during
special moments in my life, of both happiness and sadness,
joy and sorrow, and mean a great deal to me as the author. I
didn't want them to be forgotten, so I compiled them in this
book anthology so that they will live on forever, as do the
memories. Some of them were originally poems, and others
were written as songs. I put the songs to music at one time,
but realized the words were what mattered most to me. I
wanted other people to enjoy these special words, so I
decided to publish a free eBook. My only request is that
you ask my permission before using my work, and please
check out my other books for sale through Amazon.com

THANK YOU! Kathleen Morris

Table of Contents

CHAPTER ONE – BIRTHDAYS

THE DAY YOU WERE BORN
The day you were born, angels lighted the skies, They danced around with great surprise,
And brought out the sun to shine for you,
Doing what God had told them to do.
They blew their trumpets right through the cloud, Wanted to show how much they were proud. Dancing around with colors so bright,
They sang with passion and great delight.
Yes, the day you were born, all time stood still. For your mom and dad, your birth was a thrill.
A blessing much more than words can say,
Yes, God had planned for your birthday today. The very second you opened your eyes,
God made sure that you were very wise.

He planned success right from the start,
And made very sure you had a great big heart.
Oh the day you were born was wonderous and true; A one-of-a-kind made birthday for you.
This wonderful day will forever mark history;
For you will always be its most cherished mystery. So remember this day as never before,
Celebrate your birth because it's much much more. It's a special moment of love just for you,
A moment in time when you were brand-new!

BIRTHDAY FRIEND
Happy birthday to a friend who always wears a smile, who lends a cheerful helping hand and goes the extra mile. Happy birthday to a friend who serves the people well, Grinning at the customers that tried to give her hell.
Happy birthday to a friend who washes all the dishes, knowing they won't stay that way even though she wishes. Happy birthday to a friend who's been here very long,

And still she does her work each day, humming to a song. Happy
birthday to a friend who listens just because,
Who even though she's busy, actually really does.
Happy birthday to a friend who deserves the best today,
So happy birthday friend, you're more than words can say!

HAPPY BIRTHDAY BRO
My brother is a special guy,
His birthday is today.
He cares and laugh and loves a lot, and makes me feel okay.

We stick together just like glue, even though we fight.
At times we battle every day, And try to prove who's right. But
he will always be my pal, A friend along the way.

Not just on his birthday now, But every single day.
Happy birthday bro!

BIRTHDAY WISHES
Happy birthday wishes now,
On this your special day.
May you experience the best,
In every kind of way.
With blessings tailor-made for you, and happiness galore.
I hope this birthday comes complete, With many many more.

BRAIN FREEZE

Too many problems and not enough cash,
So you jumped in your hot tub with a great big splash. Instead, it
was cold and you started to freeze.
Your brain went numb so the dog barked, "Please!"
He wanted a swim and you were like snow,
So the dog got his way even though you yelled, "No!"
You shivered and fret to a time long ago,
When life was easy and you simply said, "So!"
Who would even know, what you're big dog did,
And nobody would blame you, cause you're just a kid;
A kid that tore his favorite coat,

And then blamed his sister, the perfect scapegoat.
No, nobody would bother to give you the blame.
Your knew how to tell a lie that would put anyone to shame. You
could rip apart motors on the living room floor,
And even punch holes right through the door.
It's good to be young, without any cares.
Aren't you glad you have no gray hairs?
Wait a minute, something is wrong!
They're calling your name and singing a song.
Forty years old, no that isn't right.
Just the other day you were flying a kite.
Suddenly boom, the dog licked your face.
Your brain woke up from another place.
You really are forty, and this was a dream.
You just got brain freeze from eating ice cream.
HAPPY BIRTHDAY!

BIRTHDAY CLOWN Send all the clowns,
Bring on the cake.
For today is your birthday, Make no mistake.

LITTLE GUY
Happy birthday little guy,
On this your special day.
May you enjoy the very best,
In every kind of way.
With blessings only meant for you, and happiness galore,
I hope this birthday comes complete, With many many more.

ONE
My baby is one,
She grew too fast.
She was once so small, and now that's passed.
I cherish the memories, Of the day she was born.

The tiny little slippers,
That are now old and worn.
But we must look on;
My baby must grow.

To a pretty young woman,
And leave home someday, I know.

TWO
Living and learning,
She copies me.
She does what I do,
And I love her you see. Each day she grows,
She makes me smile.
I'll cherish the memories, For she's only two,
For just a little while.

THREE
Who is my girl,
And what can she do?
She's a big girl now,
And can talk a lot to.
She can count;
She can sing;
And do almost anything. She's a kind little girl,
And loves her brother too. Happy birthday number three!

FOUR
My little girl,
She looks like me;
She talks like me;
She is a part of me.
I love her laugh;
I love her smile.
I think she's so special, Especially today.

FIVE
Happy birthday my girl;
Were so proud of you.
Today you are five,
And what can you do?
So many things;
You're a big girl now.
And soon you're starting school; My sweetheart, wow!

NUMBER ONE

This is for you my dear,
My sweet little man;
My baby, my boy;
He's grown as fast as he can. Now one-year-old;

You can't catch him if you try. He runs all over the house, Like a
butterfly.
It's hard to believe,

My boy was so small.
He fit in my tummy,
And now he's big and tall. I love you my boy!

THE SECOND
Each day unfolds,
Another tomorrow.
Time flies by,
It's such a sorrow.
Babies grow up;
We can't stop them you know. My sweet little boy;
He just has to grow.
Today he is two,
But that's okay.
I'll still hug him and kiss him, and remember this day.

NUMBER THREE
Monster trucks and little cars;
Choo choo trains and great big stars;
They are the things that make little boys;
Not the size of their shoes, but the size of their toys. A laugh and
a kiss and a snuggle up tight,
Are three more things to his delight.
What a child he is, and a man he will be;
But for now, for this year, my little boy is three.

BIG FIVE
Now you're five,

And soon off to school; You're a big boy now;
You once were so small,
In a little diaper,
And now you're growing.
I love you son!
You are still my sweetheart!

BIRTHDAY
From the time the sun gets up, Until the moon is out,

Your day will be so special,
That's what birthdays are all about. So enjoy the fun and
laughter, Play the whole day through. Remember it is your day,
When we celebrate YOU.
HAPPY BIRTHDAY!

CHRISTMAS

Twas the night before Christmas,
When all through the land,
Not a child went without,
There wasn't one empty hand.
For on this Christmas Eve,
A new way was won;
A way that would teach us,
Through God's only Son.
Compassion and mercy,
Were some of the ways,
This new way would show us,
For all of our days.
So give to each other;
Remember the poor.
On this night before Christmas,
Hate less and love more.
Merry Christmas to all and to all a good night!

CAT CHRISTMAS

Have a purr...fect holiday, And may it bring you cheer! May happiness surround you, All through the coming year!

PERFECT BABY

My God – He can do anything!
My God – Even the angels sing.
Miracle now, humbly we bow, humbly we bow. My God –
Brought us the living word!
My God – Even the shepherds heard.
Birth of a king, everyone sing, everyone sing. Perfect baby, born in a manger;
Perfect baby, straight from above.
Perfect baby, his name is Jesus;
Perfect baby, given with love.
Perfect baby, way to salvation;

Perfect baby, new life begun.
Perfect baby, Savior, redeemer;
Perfect baby, God's only Son.
Celebrations come.

He is the reason.
Tears of living today.
Celebrations come.
This is the season;
Worship the baby today.
My God – Ruler of everything.
My God – He is a perfect King!
Born just to die, remember why, remember why. My God –
Creator of everyone!
My God – Gave us his only son!
Savior divine, perfectly fine, perfectly fine.
My God – Compassionate every day.
My God – Loves us enough to say.
He is the way, listen and pray, listen and pray. My God – He has
a perfect name.
My God – Freed us from sin and shame. Forgiving you, holy and
true, holy and true.
My God – Spirit of peace and love.
My God – White as a morning dove.
Beautiful mind, gentle and kind, gentle and kind. My God –
Created the universe.
My God – Spoke every Bible verse.
Perfectly bright, follow the light, follow the light.

HE'S THE KING
It was a lonely place back then; Nowhere to hide our souls from
sin; Except for one night;
It was so bright.
Savior – Jesus;
Born tonight.
Savior – Jesus;
Guiding light.
Little – Child;
Meek and mild;

Born for you.
Spirit – Now;
Know him well.
All of you... He's the King!
He is our only chance right now. Born to deliver us somehow.
Holy and true;
Forgiving you.
Born to redeem our souls from sin. He is our only salvation.
Born just to die;
Remember why.
The greatest birthday party now.
So many generations bow.
God's only Son;
New life begun.

So many years have passed since then, but we can celebrate
again.
Birth of the King;
Everyone sing.

He is divine and pure within.
So full of love and free from sin. Follow the star;
Lovely you are.
Everyone shout His name and say; Jesus the Christ is born today.
Worship Him now;
Everyone bow.

JESUS IS THE REASON
I forgot what Christmas was; Spending money just because;
Counting presents all for me; Wondering why I don't see,
The star, the sky;
The love – love he gave to me. Falalalalala.
This Christmas, remember, remember, Jesus is the reason today.
Falalalalalala.
Jesus is the reason today.
Visa cards are maxed right out; Christmas cards are hung about;
Sitting tall on Santa's knee; Wondering why I don't see,
The star, the sky;
The love – love you gave to me. Falalalala.

Christmas carols sung with joy;
Kids all whining for a toy; Decorations on the tree;
Wondering why I don't see.
The star, the sky;
The love – love he gave to me. Falalalala.

CHRISTMAS TIME
Christmas trees and mistletoe; Children playing in the snow;
Lights of color twinkle bright; Tell us of that wondrous night;
A night so very long ago;
When Shepherds saw a star aglow; A star of wonder up above;
Telling us of God's true love.
His love was sent for every soul; Forgiveness was His only goal;

To set us free from sin and shame; To tell us Jesus is His name.
MERRY CHRISTMAS!

CHAPTER THREE – MOTHERS DAY

PRECIOUS MOTHERHOOD
Precious is the memory of when it all began;
Precious is the moment that a woman can.
Precious is the season she can hold her child;
Precious is the cooing soft and meek and mild. Precious is the
moment when she sees her children fly; Precious is the memory
of the days gone by.
Precious is the season mothering is done;
Precious is the grandma playing in the sun.

HAPPY MOTHER'S DAY The colors of the rainbow; Flowers
in bloom. Sunshine at harvest; Laughter in the room. These are
all you mom; You radiate love.

Your warmth and devotion, Is straight from above

MY MOTHER
You are my flower so beautiful and fair;
You smile at me when I'm unaware.
You put yourself last when you should be first, And you hold me
tight when I've been the worst. Yes, you are thoughtful in all that
you do;
Your gentle spirit has always been true.
You love me so softly and care every day; Mother I'm thankful
you love me this way.

MY THREE LITTLE MIRACLES
How can I thank you for the privilege to be,
A mother every day;
To teach my child to pray.
A mother,
A mother.
Lord, I'm proud to be a mother every single day; Much more

than words can say;
You bless me every day.
I thank you for my miracles today.
I thank you for my miracles today.
Nothing will replace the kind of memories you gave; A laugh, a hug, a smile;
Protector for a while.
A mother,

A mother.
When I hold them in my arms, and tell them it's all right, and gently dry their tears, And thank Him for the years; A mother,
A mother.
Growing up and growing old, I think that I'm all done.
Now they don't need me;
But I will always be,
A mother,
A mother.

FATHER'S DAY

A truck, a trailer, a great big boat,
A one-of-a-kind made leather coat.
A 454 engine for your project truck,
And shooting a prize-winning trophy buck. Yes, Dad I know that you want a lot,
But dollars and cents is what I haven't got. So, you'll have to put up with a little of this: My absolutely free Father's Day kiss!

DAD TIME

Time for a break from all that you do, Time for fishing with you know who. Time to catch the biggest fish,
Time for a Happy Father's Day wish. Time to relax and do nothing at all, Time to play a game of ball.
Time to enjoy a fun filled day,
Time for a hug in my own special way. HAPPY FATHERS DAY DAD!

FATHER'S HAND

The weathered shacks that fill the land, remind me of my father's hand.
Worn and tough from days gone by; Cracks that make you wonder why. This once impressive sagging place, reminds me of my father's face.
Full of memories so dear;
An open face to yesteryear.
The tattered windows torn apart, Remind me of my father's heart.
Open wide for all to see,
Always showing sympathy.
This exhausted place for all to peer,

Reminds me of my father dear. Wearing out his every glove;
Forever pouring out his love. Happy Father's Day!

FOREVER DAD

He works on the farm forever it seems,
And doesn't even know what a day off means.
He drives a tractor from sun up to sundown,
And the thought of retiring just makes him frown.
If you ask him to come in for a bite to eat,
He won't even rest those weary big feet.
No, if you want to see a man work as hard as he can, You won't find one more suitable than my old man. HAPPY FATHERS DAY DAD!

MY DAD

Like the mountain strong and unyielding, Vigorous, steady, and sure;
Like the snow-white peaks of grandeur, Seasoned, wise, and mature.
You've been a father of prominent strength; Always there for me. Throughout the tested course of time,
You love me unconditionally.
THANK YOU DAD!

THE HEART OF SUCCESS

The heart of success, the man of the day; The love of my life, is my dad today.
He held me tight, when I was so small; Realized then that he had it all.
A millionaire, yes, in so many ways;
His riches he shared with me so many days. Now it's my time to give back to you;
I love you daddy for loving me to.
HAPPY FATHERS DAY DAD!

MY HUSBAND

You are my life, inside and out;
You make me smile when I want to pout.
You make me laugh when I feel like crying;
You cheer me up when I feel like dying.
You are my rainbow, colorful and bright,
Your colors they shine in the dark of night.

They twinkle and glitter, they're just like gold;
My sweet little teddy bear, I just want to hold.
You are my morning, my midafternoon;
You are my evening, underneath the moon.
You make my day special, when you hold my hand, When you
kiss me softly, when you understand.

You are my star, twinkling in the sky,
You make me shiver, I don't know why.
You give me a feeling, I never had before,
I don't know what it is, I just want it more. You are my heartbeat
I feel in my chest;
When you hold me close, you can hear it best. It hurts when you
hurt, and you hurt when I do but listen to it closely, it's beating
for you.

CHAPTER FIVE – BABY

MEMORIES
If I could go back,
And relive the day,
When my baby was born,
I'd go today.
If just to remember,
The soft of your skin,
The coo of your voice,
Or the small of your chin. When placed on my tummy, my baby
and me;
Your soft suckling lips,
I wish I could see.
Just for a while,
Not to stay too long,
Cause the day you were born, Has come and gone.
Now is the future,
The present not past,
So I'll cherish the memories, And make them last.

WHAT LITTLE BOYS ARE MADE OF Muscles, sweat, and
dirty knees; Choo-choo trains and tractors.
Great big trucks and hot rod cars; Dinosaurs and rattlers.

A smile, a smirk, a little grin; Marbles on the floor.
The blessings of a baby boy, Are yours forever more!

WHAT LITTLE GIRLS MADE OF Barbie dolls and pretty
bows; Lipstick on the wall.
Perfume smelling up the room; Shopping at the mall.

A wink, a smile, a little blush; Bubbles on the floor.
The blessings of a baby girl;

Are yours forever more! CONGRATULATIONS!

SING WITH ME
ABC, 123, want to come and sing with me? 1234, shut the big door.
5678, wait!
I don't want to be late late late!
Don't want to be late late late!
I don't want to be late!

HAPPY FACE
Happy happy, put a smile on your face. Happy happy, make your heart a happy place!

SUNSHINE
Sunshine makes us warm; Makes us warm;
Make us warm.
Sunshine makes us warm; Make us warm today. Sunshine gives us light; Gives us light;
Gives us light.
Sunshine gives us light; Gives us light today. Sunshine makes things grow; Makes things grow;
Makes things grow. Sunshine makes things grow; Makes things grow today.

THANKFUL
Thankful thankful, I am thankful. Thankful thankful, yes, I am.
Thankful thankful, I am thankful. I am thankful for my friends.

LIKE A CHILD
Like a little child full of love and tender care;
She told about her Savior in her heart and pointed there.
You need to know my Jesus just the way that I now do;
Please why don't you understand, that He can love you too.
Faith just like a little child, just open up your heart;
Just believe it's simple, and make a brand-new start;
You can be so smart, if you ask Him in your heart;
Like a child.
Don't laugh at me, she said to them with tiny little tears;
She didn't really understand they didn't want to hear.
Making jokes and ridicule, she kept on witnessing;

A heart of courage and of love, the message that she would
bring.

I told her not to cry when they rejected Christ our Lord; Maybe
they'd remember who this little girl adored.
When the days are really bad, and they think back to you; They
might wish they had this faith, like little children do!

NOAH AND ME
In went the animals two by two;
Mommy and daddy and me.
"Stop over there," said the funny old guy; "Uh oh! He's talking to
me."
Noah's talking, Noah's talking to me;
Noah's talking, Noah's talking to me.
Noah's talking to me;
Noah's talking to me.
He said, "Let's go, in a hurry young pup;
We gotta get out here.
You know the rules, it's two by two,
So pick a little friend my dear."
Pulling a bunny, I dragged him along.
"This could be my partner you see."
But Noah said, "No, better leave him alone. You better come
along with me."
I jumped in his arm and then I licked his face; He smiled as he
hugged me tight.
We traveled all around the boat that day,
And then Noah kissed me good night.
"Just wait," Noah said, "before you go,
I have a little friend for you.
Found a pretty puppy, and she was alone. Maybe you and her
could be two."

TO MY BABY
We waited so long for you my dear,
And now that you are finally here,
I have so much I want to say,
And oh so much I want to pray.

But mostly I just want you to know,
About our Savior who loves you so.
He's in my heart I want Him in yours,
To fight the battles and win the wars.
Oh my child that God has given me,
I want to help in your life to see.
If I could make our home just right,
I'd keep Christ at the head both day and night. I dedicate my life to making this true,
And I promise to teach Christ-like love to you. So that when you grow up someday, I'll see, the man that Christ has meant you to be.

RAIN
People say they don't like rain;

People say it's cold.
People say it makes them sad,
But I love the rain.
It tickles my face when it falls and me; Makes me giggle and wiggle with glee; Gets me wet but I don't care;
I just want to play out there,
Because I love the rain.

BIG SHOT
I am a big shot;
Muscles I already got.
Too tough to pray;
I'll do it my way;
I'll do it my way.
Some people think strength, Just comes from within; Some people think wealth, Can pay for their sin.
Some people think life,
Is something they own,
But without God,
A big shot's alone.
I am a big shot;
Wisdom I already got. Don't try to preach;
Don't try to teach;

Don't try to teach.
I am a big shot;
Fortune I already got. Needy I'm not,
Cause I got a lot;
I got a lot.

CHAPTER SIX – FRIENDS

FRIENDS
For every time you've been there, When I needed you.
For all the ways you've shown me, What a friend can do.
For each and every moment,
You laughed along with me.
For never disappointing,
Like a friend should be.
For always understanding, Everything I say.
I really want to thank you,
For blessing me this way.

THANK YOU

I think you deserve credit for all the work you've done;
For every time you labored when we were having fun;
For all the endless hours you manicure the grass;
I think you deserve credit for a guy with so much class.
No, words alone cannot express our gratitude to you;
For all the times you lent a hand because you wanted to;
For giving up your own time when we didn't even ask;
No, words alone cannot express how well you do your task. Yes,
if we could give a medal to our favorite hardworking guy, we'd
give you a gold one today, without even asking why.
You saved us from the many skunks that hung around the tree;
Yes, if we could give a medal it would be as gold as it could be.
We appreciate the things you do, throughout the town each day;
And for taking care of all the roads so we can find our way;

For giving of your friendship to anyone in need;
We appreciate the things you do – appreciate indeed!

RELAX
I know you're real busy, always on the go.
Work work working, working to and fro.

But now it's the time,
To tell you I care.
I'm worried about you, And the burdens you bear. So stop and relax,
You deserve a break.
Go have some fun,
For goodness sake.

GRADUATION
Now you're facing the highway of life,
Your future has just begun.
You'll probably have some bumps in the road, But don't let that make you run.
Just take your time at each thing you do, Enjoy every step of the way.
And don't you forget to have fun in your life, Especially this graduation day.

GET WELL SOON These flowers are for you, to bring you good cheer. To make you forget,
All your problems dear. So, smile today,
And don't feel so blue. Before you know it, you'll be good as new.

HAPPY HOUSE WARMING You have a wonderful home, Full of beauty and charm. Make sure you treat it right, and put in a fire alarm.

Keep it tidy and clean,
And don't let the mice move in. Congratulations on your home, Now let the party begin.

KICK THE HABBIT
A smoke – a drag,
A deep inhale,
Made you cough,
Your heath to fail. BUTT – now you know, you're wise enough, you've realized,

It's not cool to puff!

SORRY
So – so – sorry,
I must admit,
I just went nuts,
A little bit.
You were right, I've got to say,
I'm very sorry,
IS THAT OKAY?

NOBODY'S FRIEND
Hopeless doubt, too tired to care;
Lost the battle that wasn't there.
Inside, outside, everything is fine; Happiness abounds beyond
the line.
Manic roller coaster, it hits again;
Down I go with the hidden pain.
Back and forth, but nobody cares; Stranded, forgotten, on the
escalator stairs. Everything is normal, except the mind;
It plays tricks on me and leaves me behind. Bit by bit, the friends
they go;
Turning their backs as if they know.
At each new turn, my life repeats;
The days, the hours, the old defeats.
When will it stop? When will it stay? When will this misery just
go away?

EASTER

Jesus hung on the cross that day,
The day he suffered and died.
He took all the filthy sins of the world,
And bled from a gash in his side.
He paid for the wrongs we all have done, And took our sins away.
He provided a path to eternal life,
In hopes that we choose Him today.
He wants us all to remember Him,
And accept his gift right now.
He said He's the way, the truth, and the life, The Bible will tell you how.
HAPPY EASTER!

WEDDING
Together you start your lives as one,
May your journey be as bright as the midday sun. May you always remember your wedding day,
As if it were something you'd never put away. Today, the beginning of husband and wife;
May you both find happiness in your married life. May your love evolve to the purest form,
So your lives together will be nothing but warm.
CONGRATULATIONS ON YOUR MARRIAGE!

CHAPTER NINE –
SYMPATHY/ENCOURAGEMENT

SYMPATHY
When you have no hope left inside, and everything falls apart,
Just reach out and call His name; God can touch your heart.
He will lift you from the depths, And pick you up to stand.
He will show you which way to go, And even hold your hand.

THROUGH IT ALL
Through the sunshine and the rain; Through the sorrow and the
pain; Through the hard things you must do; Love will always be
there too. Through the clouds a great despair; Through the losses
you must bear; Through the sorrow that you feel; Love is still so
very real.
Through his disappointing day; Through the most unusual way;
Through the morning that you face;

Love will always set the pace.

WE WILL MEET AGAIN
I lay asleep in bed one night, and had a little dream.
I saw you running down the road, beside a flowing stream.
You waived as if to say goodbye, and pointed to a light.
It lay beyond the trees afar, oh burning true and bright.
A steamy tear rolled down my cheek - Oh was it time to go?
I wouldn't let it happen now, it isn't really so.
Maybe I could just halt your course, oh down the road so gold.
The flowing streams with ended light, would be again as bold.
For you haven't even finished, the sweater meant for me.
And we were going to spend some time, visiting at tea.
Later – later, I shake my head, oh stop you must come back.
But time was ticking far too fast, there wasn't any slack.
A voice cried out, "Come follow me." You said you had to fly.
Oh, down the road the gold so bold, " It's now my time to die."
"There is one thing I need to tell, oh precious little one,"

"My soul it will survive the journey, remaining with the the Son." "So, we will meet again one day. I'll wait for you my dear,"
"Our souls shall dance and celebrate, when you are finally here!"

CHAPTER TEN – SPIRITUAL INSPIRATION

MY KNIGHT
I need a hero; someone to stand for me.
I need a hero, urgently.
I need a helper; someone to hold my hand.
I need a helper, to stand.
I need a Savior; someone to guard my soul.
I need a Savior, to know.
Jesus, you're my knight in shining armor.
Every day when I call your name, I know,
That I will be okay.
You're the only reason that I make it through my day. My light –
my Knight.
I need a teacher; someone to show me how.
I need a teacher, right now.
I need a victor; someone to win the war.
I need a victor, for sure.
I need a Savior; someone to guide my way.
I need a Savior, every day.
I need a fighter; someone to take the fall.
I need a fighter, to call.
I need a leader; someone to get me there.
I need a leader, to care.
I need a Savior; someone to rescue me.
I need a Savior, desperately.

AMAZING GRACE
His grace is amazing to me;

His grace saved my soul.
His grace is amazing to me;
His grace made me whole.
And now I realize;
Jesus really opened my eyes.

He saved me;
A filthy little wretch like me. Sacrificed himself for sin;
Just to see a loser win;
Gave me love instead of hate; Changed my awful hopeless state;
He saved me;
A filthy little wretch like me.
Loved me when I couldn't love;
Gave me wings just like a dove; Showed me His forgiving face;
When all I was, was a hopeless case. He saved me;
A filthy little wretch like me.
That's amazing grace for me;
When I was saved from misery; When Jesus Christ redeemed my
soul; Amazing Grace, He's paid my toll.
He saved me;
A filthy little wretch like me.

BEFORE YOU
He has walked the path alone, before you;
Slayed the dragon, fought the fight, before you. Jesus has been
everywhere before.
Traveled swiftly onward just before you;
Shining knight in armor strong before you.
Jesus has been everywhere.
He's been downtown, all around,
Inside, outside, upside down;
Before you;
Before you.
He led you to your victories, before you;
Sees your failures, picks you up, before you; Jesus has been
everywhere before.
Safely surely, step-by-step, before you;
Prepares a place where you can learn, before you; Jesus has been
everywhere.
There is no need to fear, he goes before you; Protector of your
innocence, before you;
Jesus has been everywhere before.
He clears the way, He makes the day, before you; He rode the
rocket, journeyed home, before you; Jesus has been everywhere,
before you!

THE WAY TO PRAY

Father in heaven, hallowed be Thy name;
Down on our knees, and we should pray the same. Give us
today, our bread;
This is what Jesus said;
Follow Him now today – and pray.
Thy kingdom come, Thy will be done;
Thy will be done.
Thy kingdom come, Thy will be done.
Forgive us all our debts that we have done,
As we forgive our debtors, everyone.
Help us to love each day;
This is our Savior's way.
Follow Him now today – and pray.
Keep us from all temptation – lead the way. Deliver from the
evil one, I pray;
On earth I'll be with you;
Heaven, I know it's true;
Follow him now today – and pray.

HEAVEN'S PARTY
When He comes back for us, He will see us smile.
Then we'll live forever, happy all the while.
When we meet in heaven, we'll be dancing in the rain – singing
Jesus' name. Heaven's party – yes I'll be there;
Standing next to you.
Celebrating the revelation;
Finally come true.
Children singing;
Bells ringing – bells ringing.
Heaven's party, it will be the best.
Heaven's party, it will be the best.
If you trust in Jesus, He will take your hand;
Lead us on to freedom – to the promise land.
Angels will be waiting, singing once again.
When we meet in heaven, we'll be dancing in the rain – singing
Jesus' name. If you want to enter into heaven's gate,
You must follow Jesus - learn to love not hate.

Soon we will be leaving, on the golden train,
Then we'll meet in heaven, we'll be dancing in the rain – singing
Jesus' name.

PERFECT
Perfect Father,
Sweet in every way.
Holy Savior,
Loves me every day.
He is my friend;
I love Him so;
I follow Him,
Wherever He goes,
Because I love him so much – oh oh. Perfect Jesus,

Pure in every way. Righteous Spirit, Loves me every day.
Gracious Ruler, Cares in every way. Sinless Shepherd, Loves me
every day.

WHEN YOU'RE DOWN
When you're down down on a sunny day,
And nothing seems to go your way;
When you're down down and feeling blue,
And rainy clouds just cover you;
When you down down on a sunny day,
Then He can take your clouds away.
Jesus, He is the King of Kings and Lord above; Perfect, He is
because he gave us His love,
In times of need and sorrow;
He'll be with us tomorrow;
So – smile...when you down.
Sunshine, He warms us with whenever were cold; Caring, He is
when we just need someone to hold; When our spirit's slowly
dying;
He'll kiss away the crying;
So – smile...when you down.
Courage, He gives us to hold our heads up high; Angels, He
guards us with will teach us how to fly; When our wings are
weak and broken;

We will hear the words He spoken;
So – smile...when you down.

RAPTURE
When will finally take us home;
He promised that he would;
To heaven where the angels are; Where all is well and good.
We've waited every day to see;
If this will be the last.
The answer that we're waiting for,
Is written in the past.
And He will come, and He will come; And He will come, and
He will come; Christ will come;
Christ will come.
The world's so very far from God;
We see it every day;
The schools, the churches, falling fast, Are taking God away.
We hold to Christ in all we do;
Await the final ride.
We try to run away from sin,

But there's nowhere left to hide. The end, the last, the finish line;
It's just around the bend.
If only all the lost could see, We're almost at the end.

So soon the time, it will arrive, when we will see the Son.
Just listen for the trumpet sound, the blessed hope will come.

RESCUE ME
Rescue me from all the misery;
From hate and cruelty;
Sadness and fear.
Rescue me from all the agony;
Send in your cavalry;
Please save me now.
And rescue me;
Please save me now,
And rescue me.
Running and a running, and a running, and a running away;

Running and a running, and a running, and a run all day.
Can't find anyone or anything to make me feel okay.
Someone,
Rescue me.
Crying and a crying, and a crying, and a crying tears;
Crying and a crying, and a crying, for so many years.
I knew I needed someone who could take away all my fears, And could,
Rescue me.
Praying and a praying, and a praying, and a praying now;
Praying and a praying, and a praying, though I don't know how.
Said a little something on my knees, to God I humbly bow.
Jesus,
Rescue me.

SERENITY
Peace and joy is in my heart with you, O Lord. Now that I have found you in my life, O Lord, There is a serenity in me.
There is a serenity me, O Lord.
There is a serenity me, O Lord.
Now, there is a serenity and me.
Saved by grace my life was found in you, O Lord. Now that you have given me new life, O Lord, There is a serenity and me.
Love and life is all I need in you, O Lord.
When I bow my head and pray to you, O Lord, There is a serenity in me.
I can rest my head a while in you, O Lord.
Calm my fears inside myself with you, O Lord.

There is a serenity in me.

JESUS IS ALWAYS HERE Jesus is always here.
Jesus is always here.
He's with us.

He's with us.
Jesus is always here. Jesus is always here.
He's with us.
He's with us.

Even through the storm; Makes you feel so warm. Helping you
each day, Until you find your way. Even when you're down,
He'll always be around. Holding on to you,
No matter what you do. Even when you fall,
You just need to call.
He will get you through; Make you feel brand-new.

BACKSLIDE
His name is Jesus; He was sent here to free us,
From the sins that we have done.
The way was to die; He would let out a sigh;
"Please forgive them, it is done."
But he keeps on dying; dying each day,
We walk away.
So listen everyone don't walk away from Jesus Christ; He paid
your price;
Don't kill him twice.
I let Him free me; and you have to believe me,
That I really followed him.
I just turned my back, and went a little bit slack,
And now I'm falling into sin.
So He keeps on dying; dying each day,
I walk away.
He called me His child; but instead I was wild,
And I really didn't care.
I yelled out His name, when I needed to blame.
I said He wasn't being fair.
So He keeps on dying; dying each day,
I walk away

STAND AND PRAISE Father – God,
I stand up and praise you. Jesus – Christ,

I stand up and praise you. Holy – Ghost,
I stand up and praise you. Lord of all,

I stand up and praise you.
I will try once more to stand up tall.
I will trust you Lord each time I fall.

You are my Savior.
My everything.
I will praise you Lord;
I stand and sing.
I will learn to let you pick me up;
I will let you fill my empty cup.
You're my friend and I will hold you tight; I will praise you Lord
and stand up right.
I will follow you,
Without regret.
I will know you canceled all my debt. You're the reason that I
live today.
I will praise you Lord,
I stand and say.

JEHOV AH
Without you, I wouldn't be;
Without you, I couldn't see;
My life would be alone.
You make me so happy now;
No words could describe how.
Jehovah.
You're more than my true love.
You're the beat that keeps my heart just right; You're my friend
my comfort every night. Jehovah.
Forever I will be;
I'm your servant, so totally,
Devoted to you.
For always, you and me,
Together in harmony.
My best friend, all the time.
I can tell you what's on my mind.
And You will hear me through.
My Savior, my best friend.
I will be yours to the end.

WE'RE THE SAME
Don't judge your neighbor, just be a friend to them. Tell them
you love them, and don't you pretend,

To care, then to stare,
At everything they do, and how they really bother you, And you
add – they're bad.
Oh that's sad – don't you know.

You should care – that's rare.
We have all fallen so short of the glory of God.
We're the same – we're the same – we're the same.
But by His grace He forgave all the sins we have done. We're the
same, we're the same, were the same.
We – are – the – same!
Don't cast the first stone, just put it down.
When you have no sin, then you can frown,
At me, then you'll see,
That you can be a winner now,
Forgiven as a sinner in this place – no disgrace,
To His face, only love you can feel,
That's real.
Christ has forgiven us, just do the same – and then, Don't think
you're better, that's just the game,
We play – everyday.
And when you do and see a sin – our judging,
Will begin again and then,
We should cry, you know why,
Cause He died – for you – and for me too!

JESUS IN MY SOUL
I am glad you're in my heart,
In my mind,
And in my soul;
In my heart when I'm alone; When I'm alone;
When I'm alone.
And I'm glad that you can see, All the pain I have in me;
All the hurt and all the fear;
And all the fear;
And all the fear.
And I'm glad that you are real; Deep inside me – Lord you heal;
In my heart,
And in my mind,

And in my soul,
Within my soul.

TEACH ME TO LOVE
Sometimes I wonder, Lord,
Why can't I love like you do?
Lord tell me,
Why can't I reach out,
With love and devotion so true?
Teach me to love like you love me,
And open my heart to your kindness, sweetness, Love so divine.
Teach me to love like you, all of the time. Teach me to love like
you, all of the time.

Sometimes my anger, it stops me from loving like you. Lord
help me.
Bitterness, hatred, it makes me forget what to do. Sometimes I'm
selfish,

I know that I really should share. Forgive me,
I should remember,
That you always want me to care.

SAVED BY GRACE
Fairness and justice, that would have been good. Payment for
payment, we would if we could.
But Jesus doesn't see it that way.
Jesus doesn't see it that way.
No tit for tat, no remembering that;
No keeping score, or asking where you're at.
Cause Jesus doesn't see it that way;
Jesus doesn't see it that way.
Saved – saved – we have been saved;
Saved – saved – we have been saved;
We have been saved...by grace.
His way is love, He will not turn his back,
And if we do, He is not keeping track;
Cause Jesus doesn't see it that way;
Jesus doesn't see it that way.

So full of sin – we should get what we deserve. Eternal
damnation should throw us a curve.
But Jesus doesn't see it that way.
Jesus doesn't see it that way.
Nothing we do will make Him love us less;
Even our sin and all the filthy mess;
Cause Jesus doesn't see it that way.
Jesus doesn't see it that way.
To Him we just shine – we're a diamond in his hand; To Him
we're refined – we're a castle in the sand. That's how He sees it –
that way;
That's how He sees it – that way.

GRACE
Grace – I have fallen from your grace.
I don't deserve you.
I haven't served you in a while.
Grace – I have turned from your embrace. Tears of sorrow,
For my tomorrow without you.
Grace – I have shame upon my face. Served you halfway;
Lost the pathway for a while.
Grace – I have given up the race.
Wrong direction.
No correction without you.

But your love found a way to bring forgiveness to my soul. Your
love found a way to cleanse my life and make me whole, with
your grace you gave to me;
Lord your grace you gave to me.

REFUGE
When the clouds of heaven look like you feel,
And you can no longer hold back the tears;
When life never seems to work out at all,
And you've had problems for so many years;
When the end looks far and the tunnel is long,
And the light has all but gone out;
When you don't know why you even bother sometimes, And
your head is consumed with doubt;

Forget the world and all that it is,
And run to the safest place;
A place of peace, and joy, and love;
A place of saving grace.
And there you'll find a special friend,
He'll teach you how to pray;
He is the God of refuge and strength;
Jesus will love you today!

ME
I went for a drive in my pickup truck,
Had to get out of there.
Any road that I would run,
Jesus would always be there.
Steering me through;
Stuck to me like glue;
Told me what to do.
He said, if you stop running and start praying in everything you
do, I can give you confidence - so much more than you ever
knew. And I could give you peace of mind, when you feel the
lowest;
I would even carry you, when you're tired and need a little rest.
I went for a walk in the pouring rain,
Had to get out of there.
Every time that I would cry,
Nobody seemed to care.
Tears in the rain;
I was in pain;
Then I heard Him again.
I went for a run in the burning sun;
Had to get out of there.
Everyone was mean to me,
It wasn't even fair,
I'm a steaming top;
Snap crackle pop;
Jesus said stop!

SIN NO MORE

Maybe if I covered it, nobody else would see. Maybe if I buried it,
It wouldn't bother me. Maybe if I just pretend,
It really wasn't there; Maybe if I close my eyes, It could just disappear. Sin, it won't just go away; You have to ask the Lord. He can just take it;

He can just break it;
Your sin will be no more. Maybe if I bowed my head, and prayed to Him today; Maybe if I asked Him to, He'd wash my sins away. Maybe if I realized.
That Jesus died for me; Maybe then I'd understand; That He can set me free.

STILL
Still through the ages, a building stands, strong, and steady, and sure;
Able to withstand the pressures of time, the weather, and the world impure. Its ancient pews, still adorn the church, stable, with glass covered shine.
Still in use every Sunday each week, parishioners sing praises to their divine. Doors of mercy, and doors of love, still welcome, and open for all.
A light unto each and every path, picking us up when we fall.
Still through the ages, a building stands, but we know it's more than that;
It's more than walls put together by man, it's where Jesus hangs His hat!

EVEN ME
They say He loves, someone like me.
But I don't know,
Just how that could be. I'm not the best;
You know that too.
I could pretend,
But that wouldn't do. So here I stand;
I've yet to see;
How Jesus loves; Even me.
Lord, here I am;

It's little me.
Will you please love, even me.
They laugh at me, When I don't fit in.

But when I try to, I never can win. Always a loser; Never okay.

How can He love me, If they think this way?

BULLY BABY
It was the color of your skin,
That made them say,
Just go away;
Just go away.
Picking and pointing at you;
You don't fit in;
You cannot win;
You cannot win.
Bully bully, bully baby;
Bully bully, bully baby;
Bully bully, bully, is it you? Is it you?
Treat your neighbor with respect;
Never nurture with neglect;
Stick up for a friend that's needing you – needing you. Jesus
treated people kind,
With his heart and soul and mind.
Follow his example every day – every day.
It was the clothes that you wore,
That made them tease;
Oh heaven please;
Oh heaven please.
Gossip, and leaving you out;
It's what they do;
Not just to you.
It was the place that you lived,
That made them choke.
You were the joke;
You were the joke.
Lying and laughing at you;
They rolled their eyes;

You were despised;
You were despised.

SONNINGDALE
This is my valley; a beautiful sight.
Its dazzling colors are wonderfully bright. It's pretty vantage;
unique by design,
Her gentle rolling hills, I proudly call mine.

LONESOME COWBOY
The tumbleweeds whirl across the land;

A lonely cowboy makes his stand;
A dying breed this rugged man;
This coarsely leathered one with tan.
He stands alone with trusted gun;
The way this unforgiving land was won. He turns his head to
squint in the sun, wishing all his work was done.

Lifting his hat, he wipes his head, wanting just to go to bed.
With heavy chaps and boots of lead, He struggles to water the
cows instead. Sunset red, with orange in the sky;

A bit of leftover beans to fry; Past and present echoes by;
Lonesome cowboy wonders why.

SEASONS
Hard and cold crispy mornings; Lifeless, motionless, and dark.
A land that is empty and barren, With no joy, no hope, and no
lark. The melting begins in the springtime; A change, delightful
and pretty.
A new day is about to begin;
Birds singing, warm sun, in the city. The pavement is hot on the
street; No air, breathless, and warm; Laughter in rivers and lakes;
Relaxing, warm day, and its charm. The trees in their fullness are
falling; Orange, and yellow, and red.

The life is no longer living;
Covered, for a season is dead.

UNEMPLOYED
Alone in the house,
With nothing to do,
Wishing I was out there,
Having fun with you.
Moping and groping,
For the day to end,
Wishing all my problems,
Would go away and mend.
Tick goes the clock,
Another hour goes by,
There's nothing to look forward to, I just let out a sigh.

It hurts me inside,
To be unemployed. Each day is empty,
It makes me annoyed.

Sunshine in the morning, it breaks the day,
But it still doesn't make, My problems go away. It's making me
bitter, and drives me crazy,

I feel like a bum,
Cause it's making me lazy.

MY SCHEME
I knew what I was doing,
The day I caught a fish.
It wasn't just a coincidence,
It started out my wish.
You might have thought I was just a girl, Trying to be a friend,
But little did you know my scheme,
Was not about to end.
You were so much fun that day,
And I was so fun too.
We are both caught in a daydream,
One that would come true.

You didn't really know it then;
It hit you by surprise;
With all the laughs and giggles,
Until you looked into my eyes.
And when the sun had turned to dusk, We were still outside;
Hoping to never end this day,
With you in my boat...and ride.

TRUST
Sometimes I know;
Sometimes I don't;
Torn between decisions,
Of what I will and won't. Listening intently;
To believe and understand;
To tell the truth;
Is what I'll have to demand. Negative talk;
These wrongs said lies; Knowing when to speak;
And what is wise.
The ears they hear;
The eyes they see;
But what's heard and said;
Is different to me.
You never know;
To trust a friend;
They may say it's the beginning,

When it's really the end.

TRIALS AND TEMPTATIONS The ups and downs,
Throughout the day;
The little trials,

That come our way.
The hurt and pain,
We sometimes feel;
When God puts us through, That big ordeal.

It's not to say,
He doesn't care;

He lets us go through it, to show us He's there. He teaches and loves, through good and bad; He uses each trial,
Not to make us mad, but to listen and learn, to draw us together,
So we can be with Him, Forever and ever.

MY BROTHER'S KEEPER When my brother sits alone,
I'll open up my arm;
I'll wrap it right around him; Protecting him from harm.
I'll hold him ever in my grasp, And learn to love him deeper,
Because the most important thing, Is to be my brother's keeper.

THE GOOD THINGS IN LIFE
The good things in life are always free, A laugh, a hug, a smile,
A little time with family and friends, Playing for a while.
Simple things like hide and seek; Children's funny ways;
Giggles in the background;
And lazy summer days;
Coffee with a friend from town; Talking on the phone;
Visiting with Grandma;
Enjoying and ice-cream cone.
So take the time for good things;
It doesn't cost a dime.
Take a moment just for fun,
And make the best of time.

OTHER BOOKS BY KATHLEEN MORRIS CAN BE FOUND ON AMAZON.COM.